D0327707

Kynance Cove

The Inner Harbour, Polperro

Perranporth

St. Ives

THE DUCHY OF CORNWALL

Cornwall is rightly known as the Delectable Duchy, for it is a land of infinite delight and unexpected enchantment. Nearly everywhere in the county you are within sight or sound of the sea which washes it on three sides and its coast is broken into majestic cliffs and rocks beaten into eerie shapes by the Atlantic rollers. There are innumerable fascinating creeks of greatly varying size which afford protection for the fishing boats against the sea and an equal protection for bathers and baskers in the sun from the winds that seldom penetrate the deep coves.

Its most famous rivers are the Tamar, which separates Devon from Cornwall, the Fowey river, at the mouth of which stands the sea port of Fowey, the Helford river and most attractive of all, the Fal, which flows from Truro through beautiful woods to the Carrick Roads, a vast natural and very deep harbour that is protected from the open sea by the towns of Falmouth and Penryn. All these rivers flow south into the English Channel. The only river that flows north is the Camel which has its outlet in the sea at the ancient and picturesque fishing port of Padstow.

Myriad wild flowers, sea-thift and convolvulus grow along the cliff-tops above the crystal clear blue of the sea which is as aquamarine in colour as the Mediterranean, and the hedgerows and cottage gardens are smothered in fuchsias and hydrangeas. As exciting as the colourful scenery, majestic isolated rocks that stand out in the sea off shore, and wonderful cliff walks are the tall granite churches with high towers that stand as landmarks for sailors at sea. These churches are dedicated to saints whose names are not heard elsewhere. They came over from Ireland or Brittany to spread the Gospel. Every village has its legend; Camelford is locally believed to have been Camelot and the ruins of Tintagel Castle, remind us not only of King Arthur and the Knights of the Round Table, but also of King Mark and Tristram and Yseult. The whole Duchy is full of prehistoric standing stones, circles, cromlechs and menhirs, relics of a very early civilisation.

So whether your interest is archaeology, sandy beaches, sailing, fishing, cliff scenery, ecclesiastical architecture or picturesque coves your choice is almost unlimited and you will find infinite riches packed in a very little room, all easily accessible by car or on foot. Perhaps best of all you will find yourself in a foreign land full of hospitable, friendly folk who will serve you with delicious Cornish cream, Cornish pasties, Cornish pilchards and other delicacies only to be found in this most delectable Duchy.

LAND'S END AND MOUNT'S BAY

The spectacular cliffs at Land's End form England's most westerly point. For centuries they have been battered by fierce Atlantic winds and waves which have worn away land which may once have stretched as far as the Isles of Scilly. Below the high granite cliffs are the bizarre, isolated rock forms of Enys Dodman and the Armed Knight, left behind by the retreating cliffs. On clear days there are magnificent views of the surrounding rugged coastline and about two miles offshore the Longships Lighthouse can be seen warning shipping away from this treacherous coast. Just north of Land's End England's most westerly community, Sennen Cove, is tucked below the cliffs. The village lies at one end of the magnificent sweep of Whitesand Bay, popular with surfers and swimmers. On the south of the Land's End peninsula is the tiny village of Porthcurno with its beach of almost white sand sheltered by jagged granite headlands including Treryn Dinas, now owned by the National Trust. Nearby, occupying a romantic setting on the cliff-top, is the Minack Theatre which opened in 1932 with a performance of Shakespeare's *The Tempest*.

Between Land's End and Lizard Point is the wide curve of Mount's Bay, its rocky shore broken by a succession of attractive coves and harbours. The largest resort on the bay is Penzance. Once important both as a market town and as a major West Country port, the harbour is still well used by small craft and a ferry crosses from the quay to the Isles of Scilly. Sub-tropical trees and shrubs grow in profusion in Penzance's beautiful gardens. Nearby Newlyn has been a source of inspiration for many artists with its lively quay-side and colourful, horse-shoe shaped harbour. Among the other picturesque villages around Mount's Bay is Mousehole, once the main fishing port for

St. Michael's Mount

Cornwall. Visited by Phoenician tin merchants more than 2500 years ago, the village has a long and fascinating history and many quaint old cottages are crowded into its narrow, twisting streets and alleyways. At Lamorna Cove the tiny harbour was used in the 19th century by ships loading granite and the steep slopes which rise up behind the bay are still covered with huge boulders from the quarries.

Land's End

The rocky pyramid of St. Michael's Mount rises nearly 300 feet from the waters of Mount's Bay opposite Marazion, which is one of Cornwall's oldest chartered towns. A large part of the bay was originally marshy woodland which was submerged in prehistoric times, giving rise to the legend of the lost Land of Lyonesse. St. Michael's Mount is now connected to the mainland by boat and by a stone causeway which is accessible only at low tide. Originally the site of a Benedictine priory established in about 1044, it is now topped by a spectacular 14th century castle.

Land's End

Sennen Cove

Porthcurno from Treryn Dinas

Lamorna Cove

Mousehole

North Pier, Newlyn

The Harbour, Penzance

St. Michael's Mount

Perran Sands, Perranuthnoe

THE LIZARD PENINSULA

Known for its majestic coastline, treacherous seas, delightful sandy coves and tiny harbours crowded with boats, the Lizard Peninsula has an infinite variety of scenery. Inland the relatively flat moorland of Goonhilly Downs, with the distinctive dishes of the Satellite Earth Station, is bordered by soft, luxuriant valleys where sturdy thatched cottages nestle in unspoilt villages.

From Nare Head round to Mullion and beyond, the peninsula offers some of the finest coastal scenery in the country with splendid cliff walks along the Cornwall South Coast Path. In the east of the peninsula lying at the foot of heavily wooded valleys tucked between rocky headlands are delightful villages of stone-built, white-washed cottages. Among them are Cadgwith, approached down a steep winding lane, and Coverack where the tiny harbour has for centuries provided a refuge for Cornish fishermen on this exposed stretch of coast. From nearby Porthallow with its wide beach there are grand views along the coast beyond Nare Head.

Perhaps the most spectacular cove on the Lizard is Kynance, on the western coast of the peninsula, where the sea has carved numerous caves and arches out of the colourful veined Serpentine rock. Also in the west are Poldhu from where the first trans-Atlantic Morse signals were sent and Mullion Cove where the harbour, exposed to the full fury of the Atlantic, was built following a severe storm in 1839 which destroyed many fishing boats.

Lizard Point is the southernmost extremity of mainland Britain and Cornwall's first lighthouse was built on the headland in 1619 when a coal fire was kept burning to warn sailors away from the rocky cliffs and treacherous coastline which for centuries has been notorious for shipwrecks. Its modern

Loe Pool, Helston

successor throws its light a distance of 29 nautical miles.

Often regarded as the gateway to the Lizard, the ancient market town of Helston was once an important port and Stannary town and was granted a charter by King John in 1201. It is best known today for the famous Furry or Floral Dance which

Mullion Cove

takes place annually on 8th May when the town is on holiday and the townsfolk dance through the streets. Near Helston is Loe Pool, the largest lake in Cornwall. It is separated from the sea by Loe Bar, a shingle ridge which continues along the coast to the one-time fishing village of Porthleven. Enclosed between steep banks, Porthleven has a surprisingly large harbour. It was built in the 19th century for exporting tin and copper and importing machinery and now provides a safe haven for sailors along this treacherous section of the coast.

Breageside, Porthleven

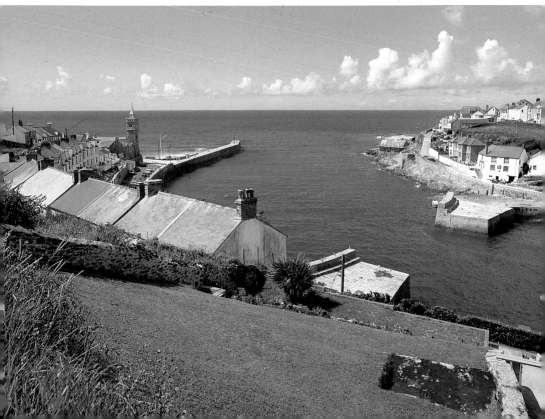

Mullion Cove and Island

Kynance Cove

Lizard Point and Lighthouse

Cadgwith

Coverack

Porthallow

Helford Passage

Helston Floral Dance

Porth Navas

THE WILDLIFE OF CORNWALL

With more than 300 miles of coastline, studded with off-shore stacks and cliff ledges, it is not surprising that birds, especially sea-birds and waders, are among the most prominent of Cornwall's rich wildlife. A frequent sight on estuaries and at scattered colonies on the north coast is the well-known cormorant and even more common is the smaller shag which prefers rocky coasts to freshwater estuaries. Most widespread of the gulls, the herring gull frequently nests on rooftops in seaside towns as well as on traditional cliff-top sites. Gannets, skilled divers which plunge like an arrow into the water from 100 feet up, and an increasing number of kittiwakes are seen all year round especially on the headlands of western Cornwall. The delightful puffin inhabits cliff-tops around Boscastle and Tintagel where guillemot and razor-bill also breed and shearwaters and fulmars can be seen in profusion in summer and autumn. The wide estuaries and sheltered bays of the south coast attract numerous wildfowl in winter when huge flocks of plovers, sand-pipers, dunlins and other small waders arrive. Herons nest especially in the woods bordering the Fal and Helford rivers; the mute swan is common on inland waters and both the whooper and Bewick's swans are regular visitors. Cornwall's geographical position accounts for numerous "casual visitors" and in autumn many migrating species make landfall in the county. Unfortunately, the famous Cornish chough is now very rare indeed.

Much of Cornwall's countryside is designated as an Area of Outstanding Natural Beauty. It is noted for the variety and abundance of its wild flowers which flourish in the open and bloom earlier than in other parts of the country. The mild climate and the variety of landscape provided by headlands, meadows, seashore, downs and moorland contribute to Cornwall's rich plant life. The delicate yellow cowslip is quite abundant in north Cornwall on the dunes and sandy river banks and the sea asparagus, another rare plant, can be seen trailing over rocks especially on the Lizard peninsula. Bright pink thrift is massed on lichen covered rocks and beds of sea campion carpet the foreshore. Several of Cornwall's sandy bays are home to the conspicuous blue flowers and spiny leaves of the sea holly while on open moorland heather and bracken flourish and luxuriant ferns grow along the hedgerows.

This profusion of flowers attracts numerous butterflies and north Cornwall is the last known habitat of the large blue butterfly. Seals can be seen around the coasts and there are breeding colonies of grey seals at Navax Point where they inhabit caves which are only accessible from the sea. Cornwall is indeed a paradise both for the amateur and the professional naturalist.

Puffins

Shag

Kittiwakes

Guillemots

Herring Gull

Lapwing

Oystercatcher

Chough

Grey Seals

Starfish

Lobster

Sea Campion

Sea Thrift

FROM ST. IVES TO NEWQUAY

This bracing stretch of coast is constantly battered by the relentless Atlantic rollers which have helped to create the wild and rugged scenery for which it is famous. Some of Cornwall's most popular resorts are here and also numerous sandy little coves lying at the foot of indomitable granite cliffs.

St. Ives is popular both with summer visitors and with artists. Holiday-makers are attracted by the fine beaches of St. Ives Bay while the quaint cobbled streets and fishermen's cottages of the old town, largely clustered around the harbour, have long provided subjects for artists. The town was at one time Cornwall's biggest pilchard port from which fish were exported as far as Italy.

Opposite St. Ives across the bay is Godrevy Point where a dangerous channel between the point and Godrevy Island claimed many victims until a light-house was built in 1859 to warn sailors away from the savage rocks. The novelist Virginia Woolf knew the area well and it was Godrevy Light which provided the inspiration for her famous novel *To the Lighthouse*. A long strip of National Trust land, offering superb views along the cliffs, separates Godrevy from Portreath. At the beginning of the 19th century this pretty little village was the site of Cornwall's first railway, a horse-powered tramroad which carried ore from the tin and copper mines down to the narrow harbour.

Further up the coast beyond St. Agnes Head is Perranporth. This popular family resort, named after St. Piran who built his first church here, is known for its magnificent three-mile long stretch of firm sand. At the southern end of the beach stand the famous Arch and Chapel Rocks. Together with some excellent surfing, the combination of sand, sea, cliffs and caves makes this one of the finest beaches in Cornwall. Nearby Trevaunance Cove at St. Agnes

Bedruthan Steps

has a sandy beach backed by towering cliffs which is popular with surfers.

On the south side of the sandy River Gannel estuary the pretty village of Crantock is sheltered from the prevailing wind between the two arms of Pentire Point. In the village itself colour-washed cottages cluster around a tiny square and the nearby beach is backed by extensive dunes.

Crantock Church

Although it is Cornwall's largest holiday resort and Britain's main surfing centre, Newquay retains much of its character as an old fishing and trading port and the harbour, which dries out at low tide to provide an extra beach, is well used by small boats. North of the town are the famous Bedruthan Steps, detached off-shore stacks created by the action of the sea. Legend has it that they were the stepping stones of the Cornish giant, Bedruthan.

The Harbour, St. Ives

Godrevy Island, Hayle

Portreath

Trevaunance Cove, St Agnes

Arch Rock, Perranporth

Crantock

Newquay

Watergate Bay

Bedruthan Steps

ROSELAND AND THE FAL

The landscape around the beautiful River Fal which flows between wooded hills into the wide expanse of Falmouth Harbour combines almost every sort of scenic delight that Cornwall has to offer. Situated on the eastern side of the estuary is the Roseland peninsula, so called from the old Cornish word *rosinis* meaning "moorland isle".

Now a popular resort and holiday centre, Falmouth was for 200 years a flourishing port and happily combines the best of the old and the new. The old town grew up around Custom House Quay which faces the river and is still busy with boats of all kinds while modern Falmouth lines the wide bay on the seaward side. Near the town is the large, reed-fringed lake at Swanpool separated from the sea only by a narrow strip of land which carries the road on towards Maenporth and the Helford River. Falmouth is the gateway to a fascinating maze of creeks and tidal inlets on one of which stands Mylor, once the site of the smallest royal dockyard in Britain. Now a haven for small boats, the village has a fine medieval church and a 13th century inn which is said to be the oldest in Cornwall. The Fal is deep enough for ocean-going ships to moor as far inland as King Harry Ferry which connects two roads across a narrow, but very beautiful, reach of the river.

Just above the ferry, the river divides with the Truro River branching off towards Cornwall's only city. Built between 1880 and 1910, Truro Cathedral with its tall, graceful spires stands on the site of an older church and is Britain's most westerly cathedral.

Looking out across the Carrick Roads towards Falmouth at the seaward

On the Fal

end of the peninsula is the dignified resort of St. Mawes. Its sheltered harbour and small, sandy beaches are overlooked by St. Mawes Castle, one of a chain of coastal defences built by Henry VIII.

Among the charming villages which are scattered throughout the Roseland peninsula is St. Just with its pretty parish church nestling at the water's edge. Picturesque Veryan stands a few miles inland and according to tradition the curious round thatched cottages were

Truro Cathedral

built in the 19th century so that there were no corners in which the devil could lie in wait. On the coast of Veryan Bay is the rocky cove of Portloe, another of Cornwall's numerous tiny ports with a slipway which is still used by fishermen. Facing east across Gerrans Bay, Portscatho was also an important fishing village but the boats which pack the tiny harbour today are used mainly for pleasure.

Round Houses, Veryan

Portscatho

St Mawes

St. Just in Roseland

Portloe

King Harry Ferry, River Fal

Truro Cathedral

Falmouth

Custom House Quay, Falmouth

The Eden Project

GARDENS OF CORNWALL

Possessing a gentle climate and numerous great country estates
rich in superb gardens. One of the most innovative of the country
is the Eden Project, situated in an old china-clay quarry near
is designed not only to display plants from around the world
endangered species, and demonstrate the relationship between
mankind. Opened in 2001, it covers 125 acres and houses 400
giant, intersecting domes which recreate the climatic condition
tropical and temperate zones.

Woodland predominates in many of Cornwall's great gardens. One of the
outstanding of the long-established estates is Lanhydrock, where
formal gardens are surrounded by mature woodland with flowering
The colourful garden at Glendurgan occupies a steep-sided valley over
the Helford River. It too is essentially a woodland garden, but also
charming water garden, a large maze and several interesting corners.

Cotehele is another garden surrounded by trees, and the grounds of
delightful house include a restored mill as well as a medieval dovecote. The
gardens are on several levels, with a formal terrace garden overlooking
shrub garden where a little stream winds down to join the River Tamar.

There are panoramic views over the River Fal estuary from the extensive
gardens of Trelissick House at Feock. Favoured by the Gulf Stream and a
warm, damp climate, Trelissick offers a wonderful mixture of natural woodland
and a shady, wild garden where ferns, bamboos and other moisture-loving
plants flourish. Not far away, at Mawnan Smith near Falmouth, is Trebah.
This mature estate is built on a 26-acre ravine where rare species of rhodo-
dendron and magnolia grow alongside huge palm trees.

At Trengwainton, just outside Penzance, rhododendrons, magnolias and
camellias are attractively contained in walled enclosures, and tender plants
thrive which do not grow in the open anywhere else in England. There is
also an attractive water garden with a succession of small waterfalls.

Dating from the early 17th century, the Lost Gardens of Heligan near
Mevagissey lay forgotten and neglected for over 70 years. Now returned to
their former splendour in Europe's largest garden restoration project, they
include walled gardens, a working kitchen garden and a "jungle" area
planted with bamboos, palms, tree ferns and other exotic plants.

Lanhydrock

Trebah

Cotehele
Glendurgan   Heligan

Trelissick

Trengwainton

FROM MEVAGISSEY TO FOWEY

Lofty headlands sheltering broad bays characterise this section of the coast where fishing and smuggling were the main sources of income until the 19th century. Romantic Caerhays Castle was rebuilt in 1808 by John Nash on the site of an earlier manor house. With its Gothic turrets and battlements it stands in a superb position at the head of Porthluney Cove overlooking Veryan Bay. Behind the castle there is a fine natural garden which includes many exotic plants grown from seed by J. C. Williams, one of the great Cornish gardeners. The former fishing hamlet of Gorran Haven, now a popular resort with a picturesque stone quay and a sheltered sandy beach, lies to the east beyond Dodman Point, a major landmark on Cornwall's southern coast and the cause of many ship-wrecks. Sandwiched between steep hills, the bustling resort of Mevagissey is protected from the prevailing west winds in the shelter of east-facing Mevagissey Bay. The busy quayside is a prime attraction for visitors with fishermen's cottages clinging precariously to the cliff-side behind the colourful inner and outer harbours where fishing boats, yachts and other small craft ride at anchor.

Close to St. Austell, the centre of the china-clay industry, there are a number of little ports which became important outlets for the trade. Charlestown, a perfect example of a small scale 18th century port, takes its name from Charles Rashleigh, a local mine owner who financed the building of the harbour to a design by John Smeaton, builder of the Eddystone lighthouse. Both Charlestown and Pentewan, its harbour abandoned when it silted up, are now popular with summer visitors as is the long, sandy beach at Carlyon Bay, eastwards from Charlestown. There are magnificent views from Gribbin Head, which juts out into the

Fowey

sea at the eastern end of St. Austell Bay, crowned by an 84 feet high "day-mark" which was erected in 1832 as an aid for sailors. It can only be reached by a footpath across fields from Menabilly which was home to Daphne du Maurier and featured in her famous Cornish novels.

Ancient Fowey with its attractive harbour extending inland between imposing headlands, is a charming mixture of old and new. Known to many as the *Troytown* of Sir Arthur Quiller-Couch's famous novel, its narrow twisting medieval streets with close-packed houses stand side by side with modern hotels along the waterfront. A busy port since the Middle Ages, Fowey has played an important part in England's maritime history and it continues to provide safe anchorage for hundreds of yachts especially in the summer months. Facing Fowey across the estuary on a thickly wooded hillside are the picturesque villages of Polruan, once a busy ship-building village, and Bodinnick. This is a typically Cornish hamlet with ancient cottages lining the steep hill as it descends to the ferry slip with the picturesque Ferry Inn standing nearby. From here the ferry plies across the deep river estuary to Fowey.

Caerhays Castle

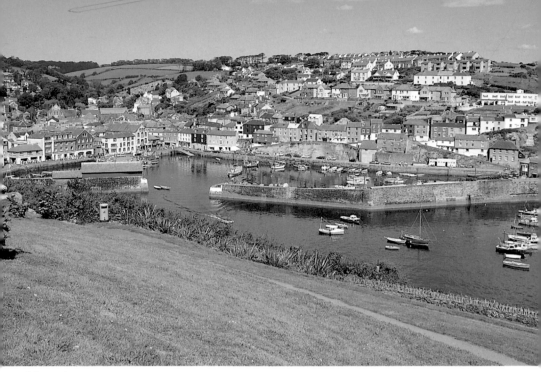

Mevagissey

Gorran Haven

Charlestown

Carlyon Bay

Harbour Entrance, Fowey and Gribbin Head

Fowey from Polruan

Polruan

Bodinnick Ferry, Fowey

SOUTH EAST CORNWALL

Between Looe and the River Tamar, Cornwall's eastern boundary, golden sands and rugged cliffs sweep along the coast. Behind them a patchwork of fields rolls inland broken up by tree-lined rivers and muddy creeks. Here are quaint old ports where ancient buildings cluster in narrow streets and fishing boats and pleasure craft bob side-by-side in picturesque harbours.

Situated at the foot of a deep wooded combe, Polperro is one of England's most attractive and enchanting fishing villages. Old white-washed cottages cluster around the tiny, bustling harbour which was once famous as a centre for smuggling but is now popular with tourists. Further round the coast the ancient Cornish towns of East and West Looe face each other across the deep valley of the Looe River, sandwiched between precipitous hills and rugged cliffs. Both townships were granted charters in the 14th century and remained independent of each other for more than 500 years. The handsome, many-arched bridge which unites them across the busy estuary was erected in the 19th century to replace the original medieval structure.

The attractive market town of Liskeard was once linked to Looe by canal and is now a popular centre for visitors being within easy reach both of the coast and of Bodmin Moor. This wild, sparsely populated expanse of granite moorland extends for about twelve miles with many rocky outcrops and ancient standing stones overlooked by the 1,375 feet high peak of Brown Willy, Cornwall's highest point.

Facing east across Plymouth Sound, the twin villages of Cawsand and Kingsand are sheltered from the prevailing winds by the peninsula which ends in Rame

Royal Albert Bridge, Saltash

Head. Cawsand Bay was a notorious centre of smuggling in the 18th century when contraband from France was brought ashore here. Before the breakwater was built across Plymouth Sound it also provided a safe anchorage for vessels approaching the port and in 1815 the ship taking Napoleon to exile put in here on its journey to St. Helena.

The Cheesewring, Liskeard

The ancient town of Saltash has a number of fine old buildings which testify by their ornate decoration to the wealth of the merchants who lived here. The town is set on a steep hill sloping down to the water's edge where riverside walks offer spectacular views of the two great bridges across the River Tamar. The Royal Albert Bridge, designed by Isambard Kingdom Brunel and opened in 1859 by the Prince Consort, carries the railway from Devon into Cornwall at a height of 100 feet above the wide river estuary. Beside it stands an elegant suspension bridge which was built in the 1960s.

Polperro Harbour

Talland Bay

West Looe

Looe

Seaton

Downderry

Kingsand

Cawsand

The Orangery, Mount Edgcumbe

THE NORTH COAST

With its high cliffs, spectacular rock formations and steep little river valleys Cornwall's wild and wave-lashed Atlantic shore is one of the most memorable stretches of coastline in Britain, full of rugged beauty and inescapably connected with Cornish legend.

Jutting out into the Atlantic the rocky promontory of Trevose Head reaches a height of nearly 250 feet and from the summit there are magnificent coastal views. Among the delightful little sandy bays in the area is dune-backed Constantine Bay and, on the sheltered eastern side of the headland, Mother Ivey's Bay and Harlyn Bay. Some five miles to the east, Padstow lies in the shelter of the broad River Camel estuary surrounded by some of Cornwall's loveliest bays and coastal walks. Its origins as a fishing port go back to the 6th century and the picturesque harbour is still well used by fishing boats and pleasure craft. Padstow is at its most colourful on May Day when the annual 'Obby 'Oss festival takes place to celebrate the coming of summer.

At the mouth of the Camel estuary there are a number of sandy bays which are popular both with holiday-makers and surfers. From Trebetherick a narrow leafy lane runs down to Daymer Bay and at Polzeath the extensive sands of Hayle Bay are sheltered by Pentire Point. The tiny haven of Port Isaac, nestling in a break in the rugged coastline, is one of the most picturesque of Cornwall's many fishing villages with narrow streets of white-washed cottages leading down to the harbour with its boats, nets and lobster pots.

Traditionally associated with the stories of King Arthur and his Knights of the Round Table, Tintagel Castle was the legendary birthplace of King Arthur.

Morwenstow, near Bude

Although the earliest parts of the present castle date only from about 1145 the remains of an ancient Celtic monastery nearby support the theory that it was built on the site of an earlier Dark Ages palace. On the shore beneath Tintagel Head, where the castle is perched 300 feet above the sea, is Merlin's Cave where the young Arthur is said to have first met the wise wizard.

Tintagel

Sturdy cottages cling to the hillside above a tiny rock-enclosed harbour at Boscastle. Once busy with sailing ships loading slate from local mines it still provides a refuge from the stormy seas along this treacherous rocky coast. Bude, most northerly town in Cornwall, was once notorious for the wreckers who looted the many ships which came to grief in the area. Surrounded by magnificent cliff scenery, Bude today makes an excellent centre for exploring the local countryside. Holiday-makers are attracted by the fine beaches while surfers from across the world come to ride the Atlantic rollers.

The Harbour, Padstow

Trevose Head

Trevone Bay

The Yachting Beach, Rock

River Camel, Wadebridge

Polzeath

Port Isaac

King Arthur's Castle, Tintagel

Gull Rock, Trebarwith

The Harbour Entrance, Boscastle

Crackington Haven

Widemouth Bay

Summerleaze Beach, Bude

HERITAGE AND CULTURE

Cornwall is an ancient kingdom rich in myth, legend and history. It possesses a wealth of prehistoric monuments, a fine heritage of Norman churches, ancient homesteads, castles and relics of its 19th century mining industry.

Probably the most awe-inspiring of Cornwall's ancient monuments are the huge stone burial chambers which were constructed 4000 years ago. Situated on the Land's End peninsula the famous Lanyon Quoit was re-erected in 1824 after it collapsed and originally would have stood even taller. The Hurlers is one of many stone circles found on Bodmin Moor. Like Stonehenge it is thought to have been used for religious purposes and according to folklore the huge granite blocks represent people turned to stone for breaking the Sabbath by dancing or playing ball games – "hurling".

Typical of Cornwall's many ancient villages is Altarnun with its outstanding medieval Church of St. Nonna which is known locally as the Cathedral of the Moor. The Old Post Office at Tintagel, now preserved by the National Trust, dates from the 1300s. This delightful medieval manor house was used as a post office in Victorian times. It is said that smugglers used to store their contraband at Jamaica Inn, an old coaching inn which was made famous by Daphne du Maurier's novel of the same name.

Surrounded on three sides by the sea, Cornwall has played an important part in England's defences. Henry VIII, fearing invasion from Europe, built a chain of castles around the coast including Pendennis and St. Mawes which guarded the entrance to the Carrick Roads. With all its guns facing the sea, St. Mawes was effective against maritime attack but easily fell to

Lanyon Quoit

Cromwell's advances from the landward side. Launceston Castle was built in Norman times and the original wooden fort later became a formidable fortress. Fiercely contested during the Civil War, it finally fell to Cromwell's forces in 1646.

Launceston Church

The picturesque villages and romantic landscapes of Cornwall have attracted many artists. A flourishing school grew up at Newlyn and St. Ives has long been a mecca with artists. In the 19th century many famous artists flocked here, founding the St. Ives School of Painting. Both sculptor Barbara Hepworth and potter Bernard Leach chose the town for their studios. It was natural therefore that St. Ives became the location for a satellite of London's Tate Gallery. Literature and music are also important and many writers have chosen to live in the county or write about it. Cornwall's Celtic heritage has given rise to a tradition of choirs and brass bands in many towns and villages and for over 60 years large audiences have visited the unique open-air Minack Theatre on its spectacular cliff-top site at Porthcurno.

The Hurlers, Bodmin Moor

Altarnun Church

The Old Post Office, Tintagel

St. Mawes Castle

Launceston Castle

Jamaica Inn

Frenchman's Creek

Minack Theatre

Tate Gallery, St. Ives

CORNISH FARE

CORNISH PASTY

For pastry
1 lb. plain flour, 5 oz. lard
Pinch of salt, Water to mix
For filling
1 lb. best quality lean beef
1 lb. potatoes, 1 lb. swede
1 small onion (optional)
1 oz. butter, Pepper and salt to taste

Set oven to 400°F or Mark 6. Make the pastry and divide into 4 equal pieces. Roll each piece into a round 7 inches in diameter. Cut up the potatoes into small, irregular shaped pieces, similarly the swede (and onion if used). Cut the beef into small cubes about ¼ inch square, removing all fat. On each round of pastry put a share of the vegetables and add the salt and pepper to taste. Then add the meat and a knob of butter and another sprinkle of pepper. Dampen the edges of the pastry and bring up from both sides with floured hands to envelope the filling. Pinch the edges together and crimp them firmly to seal. Cook on a floured tray for ¾ hour. Makes 4 pasties.

CORNISH SAFFRON CAKE

1 ½ lb. plain flour, 1 lb. margarine
½ lb. currants, ½ lb. sultanas
½ lb. candied peel, Warm water
½ teaspoon sugar, 2 oz. yeast
1 teaspoon saffron, dried in the oven and rolled to a powder

Set oven to 400°F or Mark 6. Grease two 1 lb. loaf tins. Put the flour into a warm mixing bowl. Steep the saffron in ½ pint of boiling water. Mix the yeast and sugar until runny, add a little warm water and put to sponge in a warm place. Mix all the other ingredients together, make a well in the centre, pour in the yeast mixture and mix all together thoroughly with the hands, adding the warm saffron water. Knead thoroughly. Leave in a warm place to rise for 20 minutes. Bake for ¾ hour. Lower the oven heat to 375°F or Mark 5 after 20 minutes.

CORNISH HEAVY CAKE

1 lb. plain flour
3 oz. sultanas
3 oz. currants
2 oz. lemon peel
½ lb. butter
¼ lb. lard
Pinch of salt
Water to mix

Set oven to 350°F or Mark 4. Put the flour, salt and fruit into a mixing bowl and add the fat cut into small pieces. Mix to a manageable paste with cold water. Roll into an oblong on a floured board and put to cool for 10 minutes. Then roll out to about ¾ inch thickness, brush over with milk, put on a greased and floured tray and cook for about 45 minutes.

Cover picture: Land's End   Back cover pictures: Tintagel, Padstow, Mother Ivey's Bay, Veryan

Printed and published by J. Salmon Ltd., Sevenoaks, Kent. Copyright © 1997
Neither this book nor any part or any of the illustrations, photographs or reproductions contained in it shall be sold or disposed of otherwise than as a complete book and any unauthorised sale of such part illustration, photograph or reproduction shall be deemed to be a breach of the Publisher's Copyright.